AF305213

Labyrinth

Dania Khan is a writer, poet, bibliophile, linguaphile and a quantum physics enthusiast.

Dania started putting her reflections into words with fervour since she was eight. She started compiling her work, *Labyrinth*, when she was 11. Dania is currently in middle school, but is an aspiring researcher in Astrophysics. She derives her motivation from the metaphysical world and esoteric trance of the universe. The expanse of the universe and micro-teeny environ of quantum physics lay her creative spectrum wide open for a canvas ready to be painted. She also posts reviews about the wide variety of books she reads on Goodreads (@DaniaK) and also on Instagram (@bookomaniacal). In her free time, she loves to fangirl over *These Violent Delights*, *Six of Crows* and *We Hunt the Flame*, along with the *Picture of Dorian Gray* and the *Murder of Roger Ackroyd*. Dania also has a flair for art and makes sketches inspired by nature occasionally. She is usually found lost in suspense scenes unfolding in Agatha Christie books, indulging in a hot chocolate, sporting a gigantic hoodie and ignoring her blaring writing deadlines.

Labyrinth

Dania Khan

RUPA

Published by
Rupa Publications India Pvt. Ltd 2021
7/16, Ansari Road, Daryaganj
New Delhi 110002

Sales centres:
Allahabad Bengaluru Chennai
Hyderabad Jaipur Kathmandu
Kolkata Mumbai

ISBN: 978-93-5520-014-3

First impression 2021

10 9 8 7 6 5 4 3 2 1

The moral right of the author has been asserted.

Printed at Parksons Graphics Pvt. Ltd, Mumbai

Contents

Foreword

Poems are but proses and observations set to rhythm and melody. They are lyrical avatars of words set in a harmonious motion with each crest and trough corresponding with the varied emotions of the poem. There are prose writers who never write poetry and there have been great poets who have written very little prose, but there have been writers who have done both. With a certain type of writer, the poetry merges into the prose. Their literary styles have a lyrical touch to them. With Dania's collection of poems I was mesmerized by her observation, her lyrical interpretation of things mundane or dark, calamitous and gloomy. In some of the poems the reader might find himself/herself submerged in the whirlpool of conflicting emotions while in some the reader will feel emancipated. Such is the young poetess's construct of words that it leaves you both chained and liberated, all at once.

Poems perform multiple functions. As a literary expression they tell a story; as an emotional accompaniment they weave a mesh around which the highs and the lows, the joys and sorrows of the world as seen by the poet are expressed. It gives the writer a certain feeling of accomplishment or creating something worthwhile. If the poem finds a fellow being who is sympathetic towards it, then the writer has accomplished something.

Unfortunately poetry as a literary medium is being relegated to the periphery of reader's interest and the reasons can be many. But one cause that I feel, apart from so many others, is the fact that we are living in a society which is fast paced, where people forever are looking for solutions. Everything is prescriptive, in a form of providing solutions and then quickly moving on to the next problem. So where is the time to pause and reflect on what life is throwing at you when the nearest book store's self-help section is all you need to figure out what's wrong in your life and how you can improve it? Where is the time to read between the lines and discover for yourself your own unique approach when everything is so templated! Where is the patience to get lost in the Labyrinth only to discover the proverbial road less travelled? If not the poets but surely poem readers are a thinning minority, alas!

But what is a dark cloud without its share of silver lining and so we have this collection of poems by a young writer whose lyrical expressions and profound thoughts dazzle through the dark clouds, shining like the first morning light—fresh, raw, soothing.

I congratulate the young writer for penning her first collection of poetry which is being brought out so beautifully by Rupa Publications and wish her all the

good luck in her journey of observing persons, things
and situations and giving them shape of poetry.

Life after all is in the rhythm of things!

Ruskin Bond
Mussoorie

Introduction

Anxiety, happiness, sadness and greed are some of the emotions I have poured on my omniscient paper. You must be asking, 'How can paper be omniscient?' Well, to me paper is not just a blank white page. I think paper always knows what you are going to write, it just doesn't tell you. And the ache in your heart that you get when you can't find the right word or don't like anything you've written, that, is the paper telling you that you are writing the wrong thing. The same paper knows your darkest secrets, and mine have now been released to the world.

My views are what I think make me unique. Being an introvert by nature, my own being doesn't let me express myself as much as I would like to. And poetry allows me to do just that. My passion for poetry started during lockdown when I wrote my first poem, 'Don't You'. When my mom read it, one of her first reactions was, 'Why is the poem so dark?' She couldn't believe that her child could have so much darkness within her and even I couldn't. But the truth is, I don't think I have darkness inside of me, I feel that sometimes overwhelming feelings become dark, whether it's too much joy or too much sadness, when inside someone for a long time, they find a way into your heart and become a little dark.

So, the reason why so many of my poems are dark is that the lockdown for me didn't bring slivers, but clouds of different emotions. It felt like each day I had a different cloud over my head, be it sadness, anger or joy. I was the only one under that cloud and I was the only one receiving the rain. The reason I wrote this book was to give myself a voice without asking myself questions like 'What would others think?', 'Should I say this out loud?' etc.

By writing this book, I sculpted not only a human being with a voice, but a voice so loud and so undeterred that the fact that it had a voice was the only thing that mattered. Some of my poems are related to present day problems while some are just pictures that came into my mind which I knew had to be described. Sometimes in the middle I would ask myself, 'Why do I write these poems day and night?' But then I realized I wasn't writing this book for myself, but for all the kids around the world who were about to give up. I wasn't writing this book for one person, but for every kid in the entire world.

If I was an atheist, authors would be God and their books gospel for me. They are people who seem to have been destined to carry the words of other worlds, be it fiction or not. Authors seem to be omniscient beings who know what's going to happen in the universe at a given point of time and are yet, surprised by it. I want to be this being who can captivate, string people into my red string of fate, destiny and words. I want to become a person who can make people fall in love with the character even if they know it doesn't exist. I want to make people daydream even if it's night. I want to appear in their nightmares and turn them into a white canvas for them to paint with their imagination. I want to be the kind of author who writes so much that generations to come read my books. I want my imagination to be immortalised through my books.

I have had this dream since I realized that I believe in words. I believe in words that last two syllables but fill up the silence in a conversation with their thoughts. I want to write words that are precise yet can mean anything. I believe my soul is made of words, thousands of words stitched together to form one soul and every day when I walk into the world, my soul grows bigger and so do the words inside my soul.

I want my imagination to grow like the words in my soul. I want my imagination to have wings so enormous that angels will bow down to my imagination. I want my imagination to travel to distant lands. I want my imagination to fill up the awkward silence in my head. I want my imagination to fill my head until it bursts and all my thoughts tumble out.

My thoughts already flow out of my head like a stream, onto the paper. These thoughts consume my head like voices screaming, 'Write about me! Write about me!' I do not choose between these voices. I simply pick up my pen and let my hand and the paper decide which voice they want others to listen to, which voice do they think matters, which voice screams the loudest to them or which voice speaks the softest but screams with words unsaid.

Words unsaid… Words unsaid. Words unsaid are like the demons of the heaven of words. They exist but they don't. It's like Schrodinger's words. However, they don't have a wave function to accompany them, they have nothing. But they aren't nothing. Words unsaid could tip the conversation in the blink of an eye. Words unsaid can turn the Evil Queen into Snow White. Words unsaid can make Snow White evil and Prince Charming possessed. Words unsaid are everything and nothing.

A labyrinth is often described as a place consisting of intricate passageways and blind alleys. I picked up this word while listening to the podcast 'Greeking Out' during the episode on the myth of Theseus and the Minotaur. This episode was playing in my mind while I was thinking of a title for this book. Suddenly my eyes sparkled and the light inside my head switched on as my mind stopped at the word 'labyrinth'. The word labyrinth perfectly described my emotions, an intricate passage of feelings that always ended in blind alleys.

If it wasn't for this sudden flicker in mind and the podcast, 'Greeking Out', my book's name would have probably been a Latin or an ancient Greek word that I would have come across on Google Translate.

So, I leave you with my poems, the tiny slivers of my
imagination (in between my poems), my imagination
itself and my words unsaid.

Dania Khan

Don't You?

Don't you see, the trees ignore your silent calls,
The stars scream at the sight of your malicious
intent?
Don't you see the blood-red moon above?
The grass dance with your destruction?

Don't you see the leaves rustle,
At the arrival of the cold wind?
Don't you see the shadows of those who passed by?
Don't you see the floating axe of the grim reaper,
Gleaming at the sight of new blood?

Don't you feel, the iron chains grasping your hand,
Rejoicing at the sight of fallen drops of your blood?
Don't you feel the weight of your murderous soul,
Inching away from you after every toll of the clock?
Don't you feel, the ghosts of your victims,
Looming over your shoulders every second of your
life?

Don't you hear the songs of the fairies,
Twirling at the news of your death?
Don't you hear the cry of the warriors,
Revelling at the message of your ruin?

Don't you hear the cackling witches,
Dressed in ebony cloaks dancing at the toll of
midnight?

Don't you know the wrath of God,
Burning inside of you every second as we near
midnight?
Don't you know of the silent steps of the innocent,
Coming towards your lifeless body?
Don't you know of the red stains on your hand,
The same ones that are set inside your skin?
Don't you see the midnight sky,
Ready to take upon herself,
One more corrupt soul in its burning fires?
Don't you?

An Angel

The world crashed to its knees,
Accepting defeat,
And shrouded itself in a veil of darkness.
It swept its floors of broken bones,
Cleaned its pools of blood,
And cleared up the stained rags of innocents.
It cleaned its scars,
Weeping, counting each life lost into the darkness
And celebrating each life given to the light,
As its tears seeped into the ground.

A beam of light tore up the sky.
A winged angel with white feathers came down to
Earth,
With a box in hand.
Earth looked up, hoping to be pushed into the light,
Hoping for one more chance.

The angel moved forward, an instrument in hand
And played the music of the Gods.
The music reached deep into the ground,
Seeping into every land
The melody reached the ears of Earth,
Filling her ears with a raging fire

The hills burst into flames; the houses consumed in
fire.

That was the saviour angel,
The angel who burnt Earth.

One Call

A call with him was all I needed to be wary.
The screams of the dead were all I needed to be
cautious.
The slashes of knives against the skin of criminals,
Were all I needed to put up my guard.
The bottomless eyes of the culprits,
Were all I needed to be alert.
The cries of murderers were all I needed to be
attentive.
The burning bodies of the dead,
Were all I needed to stop and think twice.
The endless bodies of prisoners,
Were all I needed to watch my step.
A call from hell was all that was needed,
To stop me from entering through the unhallowed
gates.
A call from hell was all that was needed,
To stop me from being engulfed in its fires.

'Silence is what chaos feeds on.'

Chaos

Her dagger clattered
when it reached the floor,
As she sunk to her knees,
Surrendering to the chaos surrounding her.
Her auburn hair flowed behind her,
Caught in an everlasting breeze of failure.
Her hands covered her brown eyes,
Hiding the tint of disappointment in them.
She had failed her mission,
One that could never be done again.
This was not a simulation,
It was reality.
Her leather jacket stuck to her body,
Shielding her from the turmoil outside
Her boots sunk into the ground
Her body thriving on the energy,
Of the ones chaos had not touched
And she got up once again,
Clutching her golden dagger,
Raising it into the air,
Commanding the force,
That had once vanquished her,
Chaos.

'*The answer to the universe does exist.
We are just afraid of the answer.*'

Answer

Her head sunk into her hands,
She asks,
'Am I worthy of being remembered?'

She questions,
'Am I worthy of being loved?'
She begs,
'Am I worthy of attention?'

She demands answers.
But the universe seems to ignore her.

She urges for a reaction,
But her audience seems to have left.

She prays for a response,
But it seems her words do not reach heaven.

At last, she asks,
'What am I to do?'
And she still waits for her answer.

'In this world people may live
their entire lives
searching for who they are,
while some may live through their entire lives
afraid of who they are.'

Not to Be Alive but Just Exist

The vicious comments don't hurt me,
The constant thumping in my head does.
The violent beatings don't hurt me,
The breakdowns in my bathroom do.
The knife in my back doesn't hurt me,
The memories of the dark do.
And oh! How they hurt,
They make you want to rip your heart apart into
pieces,
The sad memories infect the happy ones removing
them from your head.
Your ear-shattering cries stay within the bathroom, a
way to keep your feelings hidden from the world.
So, I know how it is to be hurt,
How it is to despise your heart, your mind and your
soul every second of your life.
I know how it is to not be alive but just exist.

‘Why do we love shattered glass so much?’
‘Oh, dearie!
It’s because we don’t want to see our whole reflection,
just bits we like.’

Love

I've searched for water in desserts cold and hot
I've touched the souls of gentle and cruel
I've seen the creation of Adam and Eve
Seen them grasp the forbidden fruit in their hands,
Laugh, as they shared it.
I've walked through valleys steep and scaled
mountains reaching the sky
I've swum in lonely rivers, floated in glum seas
I've dusted the walls of churches, prayed in the halls
of mosques
I've seen the toiling workers of Khufu's Pyramid,
Strolled in the gardens of Babylon.
I've seen the flicker of light in a baby's eyes,
I've seen the flame burn down in someone's last
moments
I've seen the love of peasants,
I've seen the sacrifice of a mother
I've seen what Gods call the mortal's curse
I've not seen much, but enough to know
That love is not a curse,
But the mortal's boon.

'They cut my wings,
but forgot that
my legs could walk for miles
till vengeance.'

Everything

They took away the wrong things,
They took away our swords, but forgot our hands.
They took away our land, but forgot our homes.
They took away our faith, but forgot our sight.
They took away our pride, but forgot our honour.
They took away our brains, but forgot our hearts.
They took away each thing, but forgot everything.

‘I want to run away from this ruined world.
But I’m afraid I’ll ruin the other one too.’

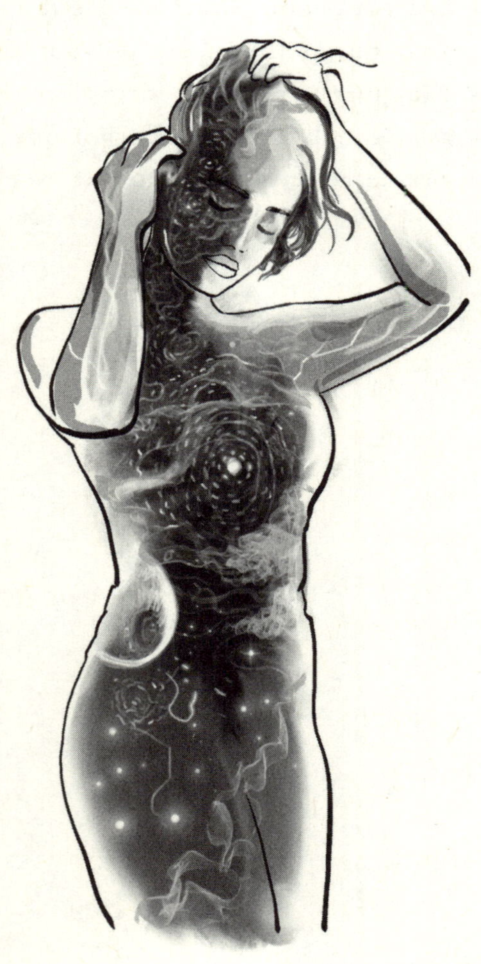

What Has Happened to My World?

As I look through the world with my muddy blue
eyes,
Everything seems black and white.
People seem to be humans,
Not black or white or brown.
Words seems to be alphabets strung together,
Not hurtful, not slander.
But as I look through the eyes of others,
I see destruction,
I see fires,
I feel jealousy,
I feel revenge,
I hear curses,
I hear screams.
What has happened to my world?

'The greatest love story isn't Romeo and Juliet
but the tale of humans and temptations.'

Don't Give Up

I swiftly follow the voice,
The constant ringing inside my head.
I run through yellow fields,
I scale mountains,
I swim across rivers,
But I never catch the voice.
I pray to God,
I meditate in a pensive mood,
But I never see the voice.
Then I ask myself,
What is this other than a useless chase?
What is this other than a distraction?
What is this?
At that moment I hear the voice again,
A string of words,
The most beautiful that I have ever heard,
The words don't give up.

'The things
we know about a person are only the things
that they want us to know.'

Dark Depths

Why does one not reach to the dark depths of her
soul?
She still covers her legs and hands to cover her scars.
She still looks away and hides her sunken, swollen
eyes.
She still hides her beaten face, thinking it might
happen again.
She has built an iron fortress, impenetrable.
To pass her days by with negativity.
She does not stand out but slowly blends into the
noise of the world,
Her identity crumbling slowly into dust.
So, ask again why can't you reach into her soul and
now, know the answer.

Greed

The sweet smell of lilies filled the air.
Her hands felt the soft green grass,
And her face warmed in the beaming sunlight.
Her mouth tasted the sweet juice of the berries,
As their purple nectar dripped from her lips.

Her eyes scanned the field searching,
They finally lay on a distant golden glimmer,
Her legs quickly moved through the field.
Soon red fluid dripped down from her lips,
Her mouth finally feeling the spear-like thorns.

She moved around hopelessly, in the darkness of the
night.
Her hand landing on broken glass.
Drops of water reached her hands,
Originating from her eyes as she winced with pain.

Her legs left their marks on acres of the glass field,
Until she tripped on a piece of glass.
Guilt was the bane of her survival,
And now it was her murderer.

Guilt had won and her soul had lost.
So, there she lay, the great Queen of Death.

Blood oozing from her legs,
Her hands sprawled across the polished glass.
Her red blood dripping from her mouth,
Her legs angled on the edges of the mirror.
But her eyes still searched, searched for the glimmer
And there it lay above her,

Unreachable
Forever.

‘Nothing lasts for long,
neither oblivion, nor fame.’

Death

Darkness coloured the room black,
Hanging curtains of sadness.
The grey sofas lay untouched,
Bearing the colour of what had been once.
The glittering ball gowns lay on the floor,
Sparkling with gems,
Hiding their holes and unfinished seams.
The cupboards flung open,
Revealing their age-old secrets,
Kept for eternity.
The blanket lay unfolded,
Disclosing its tears, hidden in its folds.
The carpet rested on the floor,
Stained red.
And in the corner sitting down,
Her head tilted was Valerie,
Her pink lips pursed,
And her bottomless eyes focusing on the floor.
Her red hair stuck to her white dress,
Spotted a pinkish-red.
Her wrists slit open bleeding into the floor.
The last of her kind was vanquished,
Death had finally conquered her.

'Depression is a side-effect of life,
but again so is laughter.'

Depression

I floated through the air,
Cured of depression.
I could finally smell the fresh daisies,
Instead of the rotten roses.
I could walk on soft clouds,
Instead of dragging myself on cobbled paths.
I could see the rainbows in the sky,
Instead of the glooming clouds.
Suddenly, searing pain shot through my heart.
I could feel the melancholy of the sky again.
I could feel the weight of my guilty soul again.
I could feel the judgmental eyes of society bearing
down on me.
I could feel the sadness, the guilt, the envy clinging
on my soul.
I thought that they were gone,
But they had never left.

'Why do you rely on the darkness?'
'It's because darkness travels faster than the light.'

Darkness

Her blazing eyes, full of fire lit up the room,
As she walked down the hall.
Her ball gown brushed the floor,
Sweeping off the dust of a thousand years.
Her red nails gripped the golden sceptre,
Glittering in the dark hall.
Her cloak trailed behind her,
Leaving the memories of the light behind.
The throne shuddered as she sat on it,
A crown on top of her flowing red hair,
And darkness in her hands.
She was the queen,
Darkness was her subject.
She was the master,
And Lucifer her apprentice.
She had been afraid of the dark,
Till the darkness became afraid of her.

*'If she keeps her mouth shut,
Doesn't mean
she has no words to say.'*

Fear

Her legs moved to the inconsistent rhythm of her
heart.
Her eyes scanned the towering buildings around her.
Her lips moved to the words of her prayer.
Acidic water dripped from her soaked red T-shirt.
Stinging her through her leather pants.
Her black heels clicked against the stone pavements,
As her hair swayed from side to side while she ran.

A certain heaviness loomed over her shoulders,
Bearing her down, into a corner.
Her face, disfigured with terror came into view,
A light shining in the darkness,
But with every passing second,
The cloud grew larger,
And the light became dimmer.
Until all there lay in the streets were,
Thousands of shrivelled bodies,
Taken away to another world,
Through fear.

'I had survived without love
So, thought I could survive with guilt.
But Oh! Was I wrong.'

Guilt

I've survived the birth of the universe,
The Big Bang
I've survived the reign of cruel kings
And buried the kind
I've brushed shoulders with death,
Fought angels
I've murdered peasants,
Poisoned the noble
I've put vicious thoughts in idle minds,
Boosted the ideas in creative brains
I've survived the end, the middle and the beginning

But I've not survived this pit inside my stomach,
I've not survived the tears of the night,
The nightmares in the day,
I've not survived the empty eyes,
The flames of hope I burnt out,
I've not survived acres of battlefields,
Pints of bloodshed
I've not survived war and guilt.

'Why can we only see light in darkness?'

Hope

I crept into the small crevice.
My eyes wandered through the darkness,
Searching for light.
I scratched the walls and screamed my lungs out,
But still no voice could be heard.
My hands grew tired, my legs became paralysed,
I was giving up.
Until I saw that ray of light,
What a bright ray of light it was.
I held it and cradled it,
Once, it grew, I used it.
I used it with all my force,
And I unleashed my love inside.
Until there was no darkness and only light.

'You dream of going inside people's minds.
But just wait till their horrors become yours too.'

Unleash the Horrors

I walk through life with my fists clenched.
Keeping my mouth shut,
To save my name.
My head bent low,
To pave the way for men.
My eyes glittering,
To hide countless sleepless nights.
My submissions to my husband,
To hide the pain inside me.
My voice soothing my kids,
To keep them from the dangers of life.
My beaming smile,
Hiding the horrors of the day.
This is my daily routine
Till one day the nightmares build up inside of me
And I unleash the horrors of life.

I Am Death

I am Hades,
I am Anubis,
I am Yama.

I have the coldest of bodies,
And the best of curses,
I have a gleaming axe,
And black robes,
I have a flaming red head,
And a pitch-black spirit.

I stand upon an island of skulls,
My blazing eyes looking for my next victim.
I have felt the breath of many,
And touched the hearts of few.
I've heard many famous words,
And collected quite a few ornaments.
I've long looked at the lost eyes of many,
Seen the darkness take them,
The flame in their eyes gone.

I long to go there too,
The place of riches and desires,
Truths and wishes.

But alas!
It is me who is cursed not humanity,
Because I am Death,
The Mighty.

I Couldn't See Myself

I stretched my palms on the glossy mirror,
Hoping to see myself,
But myself is all I couldn't see.
I could stare at the blazing fire in front of me,
I could hear the screams of suffering souls.
I could feel the heartbreak of families,
I could taste my blood as it dripped down from my
pink lips.
I could see my flowing red hair,
Bathing in the rivers running with blood.
I could hear thousands of whispering voices inside
my head,
Murderous, vile, evil voices.
I could feel my shrivelled soul,
Flourishing in this world of doom.

Land of Emotions

She strolled through the land of emotions,
Cold, like her words.
Fires scorched her like her jealousy.
Searing mists of anger poked her,
From her heart to her feet.
Her legs gave way,
And she shrieked, falling into a never-ending pit of
grief.

Her hands stretched out to the walls,
Always inching away from them.
Like her deepest desires floating away from her.
She kicked and screamed as the nightmares of night,
Came alive in this land
She walked on but dropped on the floor,
As a weight of a thousand souls bared upon her back
Her tears gave life to the floor, until she too could
cry no more,
Her soul shattered into a million pieces and fed the
monsters of the world.
She had become immortal, and her nightmares had
become eternal.

'Maybe it was me,
maybe it was not.
After all we aren't all humans,
drunk on the idea that
it wasn't our fault.'

Lies

Oh, Sire why do you not believe me?
My lips no longer run red with the words of liars.
My heart no longer beats to the drums of deceit.
My brain no longer distorts realities.
Oh, Lord why do you not believe me?
I've been burnt at the stake for my dishonesty,
My tongue has been seared under the fire of hell,
For its long tales.
Oh Prince, why do you not believe me?
My hand no longer constructs untruths,
My eyes no longer see fiction,
My brain no longer falsifies my actions.
Oh, Fair One, why do you not believe me?
For I have been tested among angels,
Seen the wrath of God,
And survived the trial of my heart.

'Why do you run away from your evil thoughts?
They are what make you human.'

Light and Dark

Red wings of the devil,
Face of an angel.
Glowing eyes, wild with scorching fire,
Moving lips, stained with blood, slinging wild curses
Onto the cowering crowd below.
The white dress of divinity wrapped itself around
her.
While the horns of the devil placed itself upon her.
She wore her crown studded with jewels from every
victim.
Her glowing red wings soared through the sky,
Like a shooting star from hell.
She smiled as the world crumbled around her.
She was after all,
The child of the light and the darkness.

'Sometimes
I fear that the bad times are not a dream
but reality.'

Loneliness

She sits there in her own bubble
Rocking back and forth,
Reciting her prayers,
Her eyes grow whiter every second,
The flame becoming fainter,
Her cheeks become less red,
Growing paler,
Her eyes wither down,
And stop listening to the minute sounds.
Her hair loosens,
Breaking away from the ties of her stress,
Her shouts of help,
Soon become whispers,
And her eyes close into the sight of a dream.
She calms down, but tenses,
As words of truth flash before her eyes,
Telling her who she is,
In the worst way she had ever imagined.
They lay right in front of her in bold blue letters,
Loneliness.

'Why do you pick up the shattered glass
even though it makes us bleed?
'Simple. We enjoy breaking things again and again and
again,
just like our hearts.'

Looking for Someone to Love

Why do we put up masks of intact relationships as we
pick up the pieces of rejected love?
Why do we search for these pieces, putting them
together one by one?
Why do we search for them,
When every piece sends a shudder through our body
and fills our veins with hatred?
Why do we search for these pieces when they make us
hate ourselves?
Why don't we notice the chasms of lies between
truths?
Why don't we notice the poison of fear in our water
of respect?
Still, we find the glue of love,
And make bridges of truth.
Still, we make antidotes of courage.
Because aren't we all humans,
Looking for someone to love?

'*Maybe it's not you I fight for,*
maybe I fight for my choices.'

Loss

Scraps of leather hung on thorns,
The owner beyond the mortal world,
Running in the everlasting green fields.
Scars adorned her fair face,
Complimenting the ocean in her deep blue eyes.
Blood ran from her lips,
Dripping down to her T-shirt.
Her black leggings ran down till her ankles,
Sticking to her legs with sweat.

Her three-inch heels dug deep into the mud,
Dragging her across the field.
But her faith rested in her strength,
She passed through woods,
Containing trees scarred with scratches,
Awarded to them by her two-inch nails.
At last, she felt the soft ground,
At last, she smelled the sweet air,
At last, she saw the purple flowers.
At last, her red hair blew with the air,
And at last, she cried, wailed and wept,
Till all that lay there was her blood-stained body,
Torn leather jacket and a shrivelled heart.

'*Bloodstains only wash off clothes.*'

Corpse

Corpses piled up on the blood-washed floor.
My red hair wavered through the air.
I coughed up blood,
As I struggled to stand on top of skeletons.
My eyes widened,
As I put my hand on top of the final skeleton.
A certain flame flickered in my pupils,
A flame telling me to wave my flag.

I climbed up,
Till I reached the top,
My lungs filled with the air of
Freedom and victory mixed with a hint of blood.

I gazed ahead at my kingdom.
Making plans of my palace of bones.
I laid down on my dead citizens,
My eyes dissolving in pitch black cruelty
As I gave out my final words,
'The regime had fallen.'

'Every man, woman and child has committed a sin.
Because without sins we are nothing, just bodies.'

Monster

Long, pale fingers picked up the dagger from the
damp floor,
The light of the shining dagger lit up the sky,
Revealing the rest of the stranger.
She raised her hood, her clothes drenched in the
endless rain,
Her pitch-black hair, a chasm of darkness sticking to
her body.
Her black heels dug into the bodies of the dead,
lying on the floor,
Their faces frozen in the phase of fear.
Her undistinguishable pants stuck to her legs,
Blending with the devastating darkness of the night.
Her blurred figure floated through the streets,
As she wiped her golden dagger,
Plunging it into every soul that she could find.
Because sometimes the world doesn't need another
hero
Sometimes what it needs is a monster.

'This is what they do,
they make weapons and say it's for peace.'

I Cannot Feel Hope

I'm asked about hope,
But I cannot deliver.
I cannot see a single ray of hope
In an eternity of darkness.
I can feel corrupt souls,
I can hear screams of innocent victims.
I can feel a million broken hearts,
A million wrecked souls.
I can hear the sad ballads of the innocent,
The constant prayers of dying soldiers.
I can hear children crying themselves to sleep.
I can feel the world, a burst of guilt, sadness and
anger.
I have roamed this world for eternity,
And have not felt one ray of light.

'Out of all the languages she knew,
she always chose silence.'

Oh, Fair Lady

Oh, Fair Lady,
Why do you ignore my familiar calls?
Oh, Gorgeous Lady,
Why do you avoid my calls of comfort?
Oh, Dazzling Lady,
Why do you pay no heed to my soothing verses?
Oh, Ravishing Lady,
Why do you reject my handmade food?
Oh, Delightful Lady,
Why do you neglect our true love?
Oh, Stunning Lady,
I will move away and never come back,
If you answer my question truthfully.
Oh, Fair Lady,
Do you truly love me?

'*Her only flaw was that she thought she had one.*'

Perfect

The night was black like a raven's feather,
And all that lay there was a sculpture.
Its blue eyes were set in stone,
Its perspective, the same as others.
Its fair face shined in the darkness of the night,
And its thin face brought shame to others.
Its silky auburn hair was tied up in a bun,
Pins of pearls adorning it.
Its pink gown covered the entire floor,
In its silver lace.
Its black stilettos raised it five inches above the
world.
And glittering under the stars was mankind's last
sculpture,
The perfect woman.

'I grow flowers of hatred, not love.'

Perishing Soul

I hope, I live,
To enter the Gardens of God were
My skin is stained in innocent blood,
My soul scorched in the fires of my betrayals
My heart is cold with loneliness that I gave my
friends
My bones broken with unending tasks, which I
loaded my mother with.
Alas! I have not entered the garden of my dreams
But the pits of my nightmares.
How I have conceded to my perishing soul.

'When I was drowning,
You gave me your hand, and I held it,
Only for you to push it in further.'

Relief

The anxiety tore her soul apart.
Her face bore scars of her nightmares,
Her pants covering the scars of her leg.
Her tattered T-shirt wrapped itself around her.
Her mind swirling with fears.
She wailed, and wailed and wailed on.
This was her curse.
Until she gave in.
Ah! The relief of giving into the devil.
The relief of all those horrors
Or had they just begun?

'To forget about one pain,
You have to remember another.'

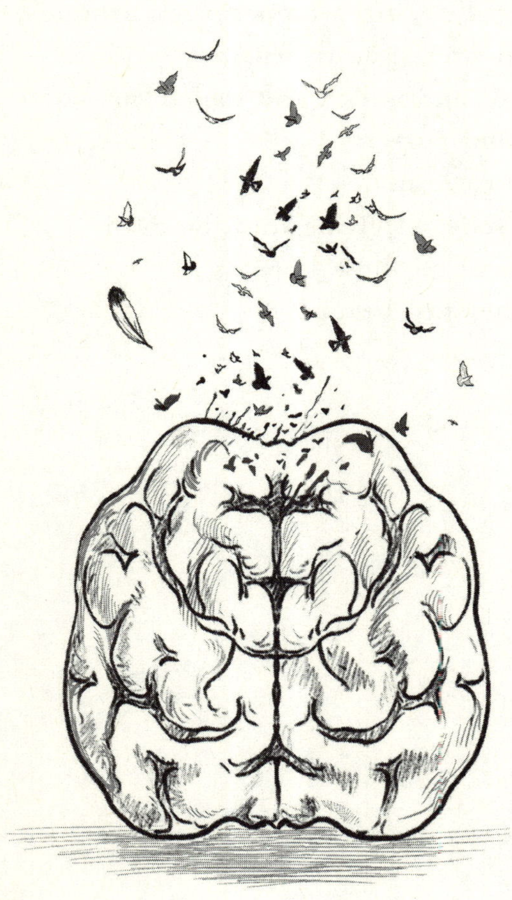

Remember

She remembers her laughs,
But doesn't remember her cries.
She remembers her green eyes,
But she doesn't remember her tears.
She remembers her beaming smile,
But she doesn't remember her deafening screams.
She remembers her soft hands, holding her,
But she doesn't remember the burns on her face.
She doesn't remember half of her life.
But she also doesn't know,
That sometimes it is fine to not remember.

'You want me to commit no sin.
Yet you wipe blood off your knife everyday.'

The Song of Life

Her golden locks reached her shoulders.
Her white dress spread out on the bench.
She pursed her pink lips,
Her cheeks sinking in.
Her pale fingers ran across the piano,
Greeting their old friend
They brushed across each key,
Bringing life to them one by one.
As she played the melody,
A white fire blazed in her golden eyes.
She went on, going to lower and lower octaves.
Now a red fire blazed in her eyes,
Commanding her to keep going.
Drunk on her music,
She went on,
Playing the song of life.

Wish

I walk through life with a wish,
A wish that I cannot quite reach,
A food that I crave,
But cannot eat.
It's a thirst for water,
That I cannot drink.
It's a word I have learned,
But cannot speak.
It's a day that I wish for,
But never arrives.
It's a memory in my brain,
That I cannot quite remember.
Alas! I cannot remember, 'What is this wish of
mine?'

Strings

He pulled the strings one by one,
The yellow, the orange and the white.
His hands touched the familiar strings,
His eyes focused on the sky.
But his hands led him astray,
Leading him towards the blue, the grey and the
green.
Screams and cries crept into his mind full of songs
and melodies of lyres.
His golden eyes turned a pitch black,
His white wings formed a matte black.
The world had been thrown into sadness, grief and
jealousy.
And so had he.

Why Do You Remember

She could still hear her agonizing cries,
And her deafening screams.
She could still hear her wicked smile,
Her glistening teeth.
She could still remember her lying eyes,
Her deceiving words.
She could still remember her fits of anger,
Her moments of sadness.
But she could not remember her hugs.
She could not remember her comforting words,
She could still not feel the warm cradle of her
mother,
She could not remember any happiness.
She could ask herself only one thing,
Why, oh why did she still remember her?

What Are Emotions?

What are emotions?
Are they the joy of seeing your loved one?
Or the anger towards your enemy? What are
emotions?
A bubble of sadness,
Or a room of joy?
A never ending well of grief,
Or a field of happiness?
What are emotions?
A fit of anger or the satisfaction of forgiveness?
What are emotions?
A constant shadow of loneliness,
Or a party of strangers?
What are emotions?
The desire of wealth,
Or unsought quests?
What are emotions?
Other than a weapon waiting to be used.

'We are products of war.
We belong in battle.'

Survival

I've seen a girl,
A girl with red hair and glowing brown eyes.
A girl who is satisfied only with blades.
A girl who is joyous only at the sight of blood.
A girl whose clothes are always torn.
A girl whose best dreams are full of dead bodies and
oozing blood.
But I've also seen a man,
A man with dark hair and blue eyes.
A man who can only survive through knives.
A man who can only survive by killing.
A man who is distraught at the sight of dead bodies.
A man who trembles at the sight of blood.
A man whose nightmares are filled with cities of
blood and corpses.
They live a thousand years apart, different in every
aspect.
But one lives to kill and the other kills to live,
After all, what is the difference?

'My hands burn with scars of murder.'

Thrill

The golden dagger emerged out of the darkness,
Gold embroidery adorning its handle.
Its blade glittered with fresh blood
As red nails grasped it.
The mysterious woman turned around,
Her black hood falling down.
A pale face was revealed,
Her red lips pursed.
Her blue eyes burned with a red fire,
Blazing with full energy.
Her auburn hair flowed behind her,
Covering her jacket.
Her black boots knocked over helpless bodies
As she passed by,
Her dagger still held by her hand,
She walked ahead,
Taking her place on her skull throne,
Drunk on the thrill of murder.

Truth

I walk through rows of daisies,
Clad in a white dress.
I run through a field of grass,
Slashing my legs as I move forward.

Moaning, I walk into a box,
And clench my stomach,
My eyes fall on a teddy bear,
My hands reach out to it,
Seeking comfort.
But tears fall from my eyes,
As it vanishes in front of me.

I close my eyes, hoping to find peaceful sleep
Instead find my dreams blotched with the ink of
nightmares
Grasping my head, I try to shake open my eyes,
But they won't budge,
They move in the barren land, far away from my
contact,
They see the bodies of hundreds and the blood of
thousands.

They sprawl on beds of broken dreams,
Paint others ideas their own,
They reveal their masterpiece.
In the barren land,
A word written in bold letters—
TRUTH.

Water of Emotions

Have you ever felt the gushing water under a tap,
Flowing like a river of feelings?
Have you felt the scalding hot,
The wrath of your anger?
Have you felt the cool drops,
The tears of your sadness?
Have you felt the sudden flow,
The gush of your feelings?
Have you felt the warmth,
The warm cuddle of your mother?
Have you felt the water of emotions,
The very bane of our existence?

Masquerade Ball

The images flutter in front of my eyes,
Chandeliers, ball gowns, suits and masks.
Masks of comfort hiding the heartache of a hundred
years,
White veils of brides painted with happiness,
Disguising the misery inside their hearts.
Doctors wearing masks of plague, preserving their
health,
Hiding the horrors of a thousand years.
The shields of knights with their daring eyes,
Shielding the pits of despair underneath.
White clothes of widows, covering their brown eyes,
Hiding the tears of torture in their lives.
The black dresses of weeping mothers,
Covering their heart,
Broken through a single bullet through their child's
chest.
I see myself, dressed in red,
Crying with the revelation of the truth,
My eyes wide open, standing in the middle of the
room.

*'It's funny how much
a little blood can affect the world.'*

The Story of the World

The music of the piano fills the room,
The musician sitting in front of it, engrossed.
He plays the melodies of Mozart,
The sonatas of Beethoven.
But as you listen closely,
He plays not music,
But weaves a story.
A story of blood and destruction,
A story of grief and love.
A story of loss and gain.
A story of guilt and pain.
The story of the world.

Remembering Shakespeare

Is it just my eyes or is your beauty everlasting?
Your fair surface hides a darker soul underneath,
A soul which is growing,
A dark soul which is waiting to be unleashed.
Your velvet cape shelters your scars,
As you walk through the court unhindered.
Each cut is a memoir,
Each one for a ruler who never surrendered.
Your sceptre holds power unspoken of,
Dark magic thriving inside it.
It holds your beauty and love,
Maybe the love we can omit.
Is it because you love no one?
No. It's because I want you to love no one.

Tears

One tear for a passion left behind
Two tears for heartbreak
Three tears for pain unbearable
Four tears for misery in the world
Five tears for an unspoken witness
Six tears for injury inflicted
Seven tears for a person lost
And a tear left unattended for a heart turned cold.

Acknowledgements

Everyone has their own perspective that is unique—this is something that I've come to love. But during the pandemic, sharing one's perspective became impossible. As they say, 'The mind is its own place, and, in itself, can make a heaven of hell, a hell of heaven.' Such thoughts were building up inside me and I felt a deep urge to present my perspective to the world. This led to the birth of the poet in me.

As I started my voyage, my parents, especially my mom, enlivened my spirits and believed in me more than I did in myself. My sister proved to be the first source of optimism and assurance. She became my go-to proofreader who helped me stay positive. The source of positivity went beyond my family, for everyone around helped me throughout the process. My family provided me with constructive criticism and helped my words reach the quality they are today.

Ms Urmila Ramakrishna, my English teacher, coached me on how to portray my inner thoughts with flair and clarity. She helped me improve with every word I wrote, by reviewing my content and giving her valuable feedback. My window to the world was thrown open by Ms Nitya Alwani Satyani. How could I forget her first post about me on her webpage! It doesn't matter how many times you get to go to the moon; the first trip is always very special. My uncle, Rao Nayyar, was one of the pillars who made this book possible with his constant support and fortitude. I could bounce ideas off him and aggrandize my creativity multifold. Sheodan Singh uncle and Vivek Verma uncle were two people who read every bit of what I wrote and sowed the seeds of my dream to get my book published. They shepherded through the process and made my work reach you as a reader.

I would also like to thank team Rupa who acknowledged my potential and agreed to publish my work.

I would also like to express my gratitude to the greatest storyteller up the hill, Mr Ruskin Bond, for writing a beautiful foreword.

I hope that you find a bit of yourself in these poems and take a bit of me along with you. Because you, dear reader, make me an author.

Dania Khan